POCKET

Frida Kahlo®

WISDOM

Inspirational quotes and wise words
from a legendary icon

Hardie Grant

BOOKS

Contents

Frida Kahlo

on...

ART

> **"**
>
> My painting carries with it
> the message of pain.
>
> **"**

ART 6

"

Painting completed
my life.

"

"

The only thing I know is
that I paint because I need
to, and I paint whatever
passes through my
head without any other
consideration.

"

ART **8**

"

I'll paint myself because
I am so often alone,
because I am the subject
I know best.

"

ART 9

"

They thought I was
a Surrealist, but I wasn't.
I never painted dreams.
I painted my own reality.

"

ART 10

"

To paint is the most
terrific thing that
there is, but to do it well
is very difficult.

"

"

I was born a bitch.
I was born a painter.

"

ART **12**

"

I am not sick. I am broken.
But, I am happy to be alive
as long as I can paint.

"

"

My paintings are the most
frank expression
of myself, without taking
into consideration
either judgements
or prejudices of anyone.

"

ART **14**

"

I don't know if my
paintings are Surrealist
or not, but what I am sure
of is that they are the
most honest expression
of my being.

"

Frida Kahlo®

on...

HERSELF

"

Feet, what do
I need you for when
I have wings to fly?

"

HERSELF **18**

"

I think that little by little
I'll be able to solve
my problems and survive.

"

"

I tried to drown my
sorrows, but the bastards
learned how to swim,
and now I am overwhelmed
by this decent
and good feeling.

"

"

What doesn't kill me,
nourishes me.

"

66

I used to think I was
the strangest person in the
world, but then I thought,
there are so many people
in the world, there must
be someone just like
me who feels flawed
and bizarre in the same
ways I do...

HERSELF 22

I would imagine her, and
imagine that she must be
out there thinking of me
too. Well, I hope that if
you are out there and read
this, know that, yes,
it's true I'm here, and
I'm just as strange as you.

"

"

I already know everything,
without reading or
writing. Not very long ago,
maybe only a few days
back, I was a girl going
her way through a world
of precise and tangible
colours and forms.

"

HERSELF 24

"

The most important part
of the body is the brain.
Of my face, I like
the eyebrows and eyes.

"

"

I wish I could do whatever
I liked behind the curtain
of madness. Then: I'd
arrange flowers, all day
long, I'd paint; pain, love
and tenderness, I would
laugh as much as I feel like
at the stupidity of others
and they would all say:...

HERSELF 26

'Poor thing, she's crazy!'.
(Above all I would laugh
at my own stupidity.)

"

"

I am female,
but I have talent!

"

HERSELF 28

"

My blood is a miracle
that, from my veins,
crosses the air from my
heart to yours.

"

"

Drink to forget, but now...
I do not remember what.

"

"

Whenever I speak with
you I end up by
dying more, a little more.

"

Frida Kahlo®

on...

LOVE

"

Take a lover who looks
at you like maybe you are
a bourbon biscuit.

"

"

Take a lover who
looks at you like maybe
you are magic.

"

"

You deserve the best,
the very best, because you
are one of the few people
in this miserable world...

LOVE 36

who remain honest with
others and that is the only
thing that really counts.

"

66

I leave you my portrait
so that you will have
my presence all the days
and nights that I am
away from you.

99

"

I would give you
everything that you never
had, and even then
you'd know the wonder
that is the power to love.

"

"

I love you... thank you
because you live, because
yesterday you allowed me
to touch your intimate
light and because you said
with your voice and your
eyes what I was waiting for
all my life.

"

LOVE 40

"

Love me a little.
I adore you.

"

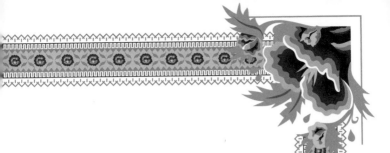

Frida Kahlo®

on...

DIEGO

"

Diego: nothing compares
to your hands, nothing like
the green-gold of your
eyes. My body is filled
with you for days and days.
You are the mirror of the
night. The violent flash
of lightning. The dampness
of the earth...

DIEGO 44

The hollow of your
armpits is my shelter. My
fingers touch your blood.
All my joy is to feel life
spring from your flower-
fountain that mine keeps
to fill all the paths of my
nerves which are yours.

99

"

There have been two great
accidents in my life.
one was the train the other
was Diego. Diego was by
far the worst.

"

DIEGO 46

"

I can not speak of Diego as
my husband because that
term, when applied to him,
is an absurdity. He never
has been, nor will he ever
be, anybody's husband.

"

DIEGO 47

"

You too know that all my
eyes see, all I touch with
myself, from any distance,
is Diego. The caress
of fabrics, the colour of
colours, the wires, the
nerves, the pencils...

DIEGO 48

the leaves, the dust, the
cells, the war and the sun,
everything experienced
in the minutes of the
non-clocks and the non-
calendars and the empty
non-glances, is him.

„

"

I saw Diego, and that
helped more than anything
else... I will marry Diego
again... I am very happy.

"

DIEGO 50

"

Your word travels the
entirety of space and
reaches my cells, which are
my stars, then goes to
yours which are my light.

"

DIEGO **51**

"

All this anger has simply
made me understand
better that I love you more
than my own skin, and
that even though you
don't love me as much,
you love me a little anyway
– don't you?...

DIEGO 52

If this is not true,
I'll always be hopeful
that it could be,
and that's enough for me.

"

DIEGO 53

"

You took me in
and gave me back broken,
whole, complete.

"

DIEGO 54

"

Your excessive passion
wrapped me: the flames
of the love were immense.

"

DIEGO 55

"

From you to my hands,
I caress your entire body,
and I am with you for a
minute and I am myself for
a moment...

DIEGO 56

And my blood is the
miracle, which runs
in the vessels of the air
from my heart to yours.

"

"

I warn you that in this
picture I am painting of
Diego there will be colours
which even I am not fully
acquainted with...

DIEGO 58

Besides, I love Diego
so much I can not be
an objective speculator
of him or his life.

"

66

You missed the
opportunity to be happy.

99

DIEGO **60**

"

Your hands shook me.

"

Frida Kahlo®

on...

LIFE

"

Nothing is absolute.
Everything changes,
everything moves,
everything revolves,
everything flies
and goes away.

"

LIFE 64

"

There is nothing more
precious than laughter.

"

"

At the end of the day,
we can endure much more
than we think we can.

"

LIFE 66

"

Only one mountain
can know the core
of another mountain.

"

"

Tragedy is the most
ridiculous thing.

"

LIFE 68

"

I hope the exit is joyful
– and I hope
never to come back.

„

"

I must fight with all my
strength so that the little
positive things that my
health allows me to
do might be pointed
toward helping the
revolution. The only real
reason for living.

"

"

Pain, pleasure and death
are no more than a process
for existence. The
revolutionary struggle in
this process is a doorway
open to intelligence.

"

"

It is not worthwhile
to leave this world
without having had
a little fun in life.

"

LIFE 72

"

It is a strength to laugh
and to abandon oneself,
to be light.

"

"

Doctor, if you let me take
this tequila, I promise you
not to drink at my funeral.

"

"

Beauty and ugliness are
a mirage, because
others end up seeing
what's inside of us.

"

"

I am in agreement with
everything my father
taught me and my mother
taught me.

"

66

Life is either a daring
adventure or nothing.

99

"

The pain is not part
of the life, but can be
converted into life itself.

"

"

The mirror!
Executioner of my days!

"

"

You have to be honest;
we women can not live
without pain.

"

"

What would I do
without the absurd
and the fleeting.

"

Frida Kahlo®

on...

SOCIETY

66

The most important thing
for everyone in
Gringolandia is to have
ambition and become
'somebody,' and frankly,
I don't have
the least ambition to
become anybody.

99

"

I find that Americans
completely lack sensibility
and good taste. They are
boring and they all have
faces like unbaked rolls.

"

66

It was worthwhile to come
here only to see why
Europe is rottening,
why all this people –
good for nothing –
are the cause of all the
Hitlers and Mussolinis.

99

"

I am nauseated by all these
rotten people in Europe –
and these fucking
'democracies' are not
worth even a crumb.

"

"

I could kill that guy
and eat it afterwards...

"

"

This upper class is
disgusting and I'm furious
at all these rich people
here, having seen
thousands of people
in abject squalor.

"

"

Sometimes I prefer to talk
to workers and bricklayers
instead of those stupid
people calling themselves
educated people.

"

"

They are a bunch
of coo-coo, lunatic, sons
of bitches Surrealists.

"

"

The devil is blonde and his
blue eyes, like two stars
fired love, with his tie
and red panties. I think
the devil is lovely.

"

"

I would build my world
which, while I lived,
would be in agreement
with all the worlds.

"

Sources

Blago Kirov (2014) *The Famous: Book 3,
Osmora Incorporated* - pp. **15, 19, 20, 26-27,
28, 29, 30, 31, 36-37, 39, 40, 46, 47, 54, 55,
60, 61, 66, 71, 74, 79, 80, 81**

Carole Maso (2002) *Beauty is Convulsive:
The Passion of Frida Kahlo*, Counterpoint
- pp. **56-57**

Camilla Morton (2011) *A Year in High
Heels*, Hachette UK - p. **38**

Carol Sabbeth (2005) *Frida Kahlo and Diego
and Rivera: Their Lives and Ideas*, Chicago
Review Press - pp. **13, 18**

Chrissie Grace (2008) *Tiles Gone Wild:
New Directions in Mixed Media Mosaics*,
North Light Books - p. **8**

David H. Lowenherz (2012) *The Greatest
Love Letters of All Time*, Crown - pp. **44-45**

Diego Rivera (1960) *My Art, My Life: An
Autobiography*, Courier Corporation -
pp. **58-59**

Elizabeth Hess Stamper (2016)
The Butterfly Book, Balboa Press - p. **35**

Gerry Souter (2016) *Frida Kahlo*, Parkstone
International - pp. **52-53, 88, 89**

Guardian, 21st May 2005 - p. **9**

Hayden Herrera, *Frida Kahlo: The Paintings*
(1993) Bloomsbury Publishing - p. **69**

Helga Prignitz-Poda, Ingried Brugger,
Peter von Becker (2010) *Frida Kahlo:
retrospective*, Prestel Verlag - pp. **51, 68**

John Bloomberg-Rissman (2017) *In the
House of the Hangman, Vol. 6*, Lulu Press -
pp. **84, 93**

Karla Clark (2017) *Everybody and
Their Brother*, AuthorHouse - p. **64**

Laura Barcella (2017) *Fight Like a Girl*,
Summersdale Publishers - pp. **24, 70**

Lawrence Tabak (2014) *In Real Life*,
Tuttle Publishing - p. **12**

Maria Tsenava (2013) *Frida and Diego:
Quotes*, Lulu Press - pp. **6, 7, 21, 34, 75, 77,
78, 90, 91, 92**

Sarah M. Lowe (1995) *The Diary
of Frida Kahlo: An Intimate Self-Portrait*,
Abrams - pp. **48-49, 65, 67, 87**

Smithsonian Magazine, November 2002
- pp. **11, 72, 84, 85, 86**

Time Magazine, 27th April 1953 - p. **10**

Vanity Fair, 1995 - pp. **50, 76**

Victoria Brownworth (2015) *Ordinary
Mayhem*, Bold Strokes Books Inc. -
pp. **22-23, 25**

Zena Alkayat and Nina Cosford (2016)
Frida Kahlo, Francis Lincoln Publishers -
pp. **14, 73**

Pocket Frida Kahlo Wisdom

Published in 2018 by Hardie Grant Books, an imprint of Hardie Grant Publishing
This book was authorised by the Frida Kahlo® Corporation

Hardie Grant Books (London)
5th & 6th Floors
52–54 Southwark Street
London SE1 1UN

Hardie Grant Books (Melbourne)
Building 1, 658 Church Street
Richmond, Victoria 3121

hardiegrantbooks.com

British Library Cataloguing-in-Publication Data. A catalogue record
for this book is available from the British Library.

ISBN: 978-1-78488-180-1

20 19 18 17 16 15 14 13 12

Publisher: Kate Pollard
Commissioning Editor: Kajal Mistry
Senior Editor: Molly Ahuja
Publishing Assistant: Eila Purvis
Design: Daisy Dudley
Illustrator: Michele Rosenthal

Colour Reproduction by p2d
Printed and bound in China by Leo Paper Products Ltd.